Negativ

Simply Ridiculous!

A Realization and Transformation of
Ridiculous Beliefs and Behaviors

by Millicent St. Claire
Illustrations by the Author

The Simply Ridiculous Series Volume 1

Negativity and Drama is Simply Ridiculous!

A Realization and Transformation of
Ridiculous Beliefs and Behaviors

A Self-Help Book by Millicent St. Claire
Copyright © 2007 by Millicent St. Claire.
All Illustrations © 2007 by Millicent St. Claire.
All rights reserved worldwide.

Simply Ridiculous Publishing
P.O. Box 1140, Lithonia, GA 30058
www.LIGMO.com
ISBN-13: 978-1497381650
ISBN-10:1497381657

Although the author hopes you don't trample on the
copyright, we do hope you'll share what you find of value
in this book with others. We'd love to hear from you!
Live! Love! Learn! Laugh! LIGMO!

Other Simply Ridiculous Books:
Looking for Love in all the wrong places is Simply Ridiculous!
Not Surrendering is Simply Ridiculous!

Disclaimer: This publication is designed as a guided self-help
book, and to provide personal insights on self-improvement.
It is shared with the understanding that the author is
not engaged in rendering expert therapeutic advice.
If other expert assistance is required, the services of a
competent professional therapist should be sought.

Dedication

To Mary Rose Campbell who did a great service
in helping me see the possibilities for my life
and support with letting go of the stories about
my ridiculous past. Love and Light to you Mary!

Special Thanks and Blessings to Dr. Barbara King
for reminding me that I am a unique, one-of-a-kind,
Miracle of the Universe. And now I believe it!

Table of Contents

About the Illustrations

For over a year, I had been trying to find an illustrator and had many artists submit drawings for the concept. The project had been on hold as a result. None of them worked or represented the ideas I had in mind.

One day, out of frustration, I said to myself, *"Hey! I just need a basic stick figure that can express the feelings and I need to get this thing done! I'll go into big-kid mode and do it myself!"*

So, after PhotoReading, *Drawing on the Right Side of the Brain by Betty Edwards* and a short prayer and invocation to the great artists of the Universe, I sat down one Friday morning and began. After a short evolutionary process, the character revealed herself. I was on a roll and completed all the illustrations within a few days.

During the process, I found myself getting a little twisted up because I couldn't make her arms and body do the things I wanted like run or sit. Oh well. I decided to ignore that silly perfectionist voice and just do the thing! Now I'm on to the best sellers list!

What the experience taught me was that once again, as in my past, I had been giving my power away and waiting on someone to do something for me that I could do for myself.

The drawings aren't perfect. Do they need to be? When I showed them to my accountability partner, he smiled and said, *"They're perfectly authentic and no one could have expressed them better!"* That was all the validation I needed to start my new career as an artist!

I hope you enjoy MeMe's evolution as much as I do!

It's funny how things that

NOW

seem so obvious to me…

Weren't

BACK THEN.

I had lots of 'important beliefs' about

MYSELF:
Who I was
who I am
and who I should be

OTHER PEOPLE:
What they did wrong and
what they made me do.

LIFE:
What it owed me and
why it wasn't working!

But now I find those beliefs to be

SIMPLY RIDICULOUS!

Chapter 1

Denial

I made up some incredible stories
to support my beliefs and to
help me survive.

The weird thing is -
my stories almost destroyed me.

Denial made me feel inadequate and small
and my head was filled with
NEGATIVE SELF-TALK
that made me doubt my abilities.

For years I had been listening to the
RIDICULOUS VOICE
of *'the other'*

You know who *'the other'* is.
It's all those voices that whisper
all of that negative talk into your head
in the first place.

A RIDICULOUS character full of RIDICULOUS programming.

After a while, *'the other'*
convinced me what I should be like
and kept me from being
who I AM.

A RIDICULOUS FACT

that I had been blinded to for years.

The *'the other'* persuaded me that I should
spend my entire life trying to

MAKE IT BIG!

and keep up with all others.

I foolishly embraced this
RIDICULOUS LIFE.

After years of listening to *'the other'*
I was
hypnotized
mesmerized &
stupefied

by a bunch of
RIDICULOUS NOTIONS.

I DIDN'T LIVE IN REALITY!

And as a result, I developed
"THE LOGIC OF SHOULD"
or seeing my life as is 'should be'
instead of the way it really was.

This
RIDICULOUS LOGIC
helped me avoid taking responsibility
for the real issues in my life.

Denial fooled me into
playing many roles, including
The VICTIM Role!

A RIDICULOUSLY
UNBECOMING ROLE

that I took very serious!

When things got tough,
I took the easy way out.

I made everyone
BAD AND WRONG
for e-v-e-r-y-t-h-i-n-g!

Denial made this easy and convenient.

And I couldn't recognize the
RIDICULOUSNESS of it all.

It was never my fault when things went wrong.
I LOVED FINGER-POINTING.

I blamed family, friends, and total strangers –

I EVEN BLAMED GOD!

RIDICULOUS to the extreme.

The effects of denial were widespread.
My personal life was a wreck.
But instead of looking in the mirror,
I focused on the faults of others.

He was too short, bald, mean, tall.
(He ain't all that! Who died and left him in charge?)

She was too fat, sassy, or bossy or classy.
(She thinks she got it going on!
Who does she think she is?)

My view of people was
RIDICULOUSLY SKEWED.

And my
NEED TO BE RIGHT
was more important than anything else.

I'd rather be put out on the side of a desert road-
and stand in cactus!
than to admit I was wrong.

AND IT GOT WORSE!

I was never satisfied.

No one could live up to
MY STANDARDS and MY IDEAS
of what **I THOUGHT** they should do
or how **I THOUGHT** they should act

I was
RIDICULOUSLY JUDGMENTAL.

I carried grudges from old past hurts -
and made new friends pay the price.

A RIDICULOUS BURDEN

That began to have a hazardous effect on my health.

I even invented hurts
and read into what people said…

My selective hearing was
RIDICLOUSLY ACUTE.

I broke promises – and then
shifted
the
blame…

A RIDICULOUS DIVERSION

to my lack of integrity.

To cover up for all the madness,
I created an
IMPENETRABLE WALL
around myself.

I was
RIDICULOUSLY GOOD
at shutting other out and withholding myself.

I felt vulnerable and I paid close attention to
what others thought about me.

Trying desperately to be liked,
I went along with the program.

No matter how
RIDICULOUS.

The one thing I was sure of was this:
I had to
LOOK GOOD at ALL COSTS!

A RIDICULOUSLY VAIN MASQUERADE.

While I may have looked good on the outside,
inside I was a mess.

I focused on outer appearance
instead of inner beauty.

To cover up for the things I lacked inside,
I spent a great deal of time in the
Beauty Shop
and the
Nail Shop
instead of the
Knowledge Shop!

And I had hidden resentment inside
and I didn't know how to
express myself in a positive way.

I was
RIDICULOUSLY CONFLICTED.

Desperate, I wasted precious time
LOOKING FOR LOVE
in all the wrong places.

A RIDICULOUSLY FUTILE SEARCH.

And I kept hanging out – wishing for that
KNIGHT IN SHINNING ARMOR
to rescue me from my ridiculousness.

A RIDICULOUS ILLUSION.

I magnetized all the wrong things to myself -
and then cried…

A SERIOUSLY RIDICULOUS ACT.

Not realizing that I was acting out
old scripts from childhood models and
past negative programming…

I persisted with my
RIDICULOUS ANTICS!

I was a mess –
FLYING OFF THE HANDLE
at every turn and at everybody.
I would both explode and implode.

I was a real SCREAMING MEME!

I was in pain and blinded by my own
RIDICULOUS REACTIONS.

Personally and professionally,
my life was a mixed up muddle.

I was topsy-turvy and I kept changing
careers, residences, telephone numbers,
and relationships…

I was
RIDICULOUSLY CONFUSED &
UNSTABLE.

I kept hoping things would get better
and that I might find some answers -

Maybe in the next church service,
the next seminar,
the next self-help group;
or the next class.

Perhaps the answer was in
a new book;
a new tape series;
or a new relationship.

I was
RIDICULOUSLY LOST.

In the meantime, the charade of
LOOKING GOOD & FAKING IT
had become expensive and exhausting.

I was a
RIDICULOUS FRAUD
and I was heavy laden with DUKKHA
(suffering, drama and negativity).

I was forever gullible to the
'NEXT BIG THING'
that would put me over the top
and help me get rich.

I put a
**RIDICULOUS AMOUNT OF TIME
AND ENERGY**
into programs and never got
what I really wanted or needed.

At times my life seemed like one big
networking marketing event.

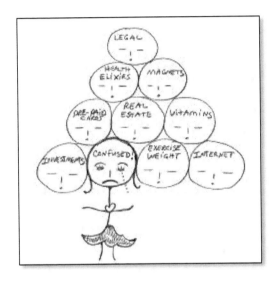

My commitment was weak,
my energy was scattered
and I was lost in the sauce. I felt
RIDICULOUSLY INEFFECTIVE.

The opportunities ALL sounded good and
I didn't want to miss the boat!

I didn't know how to say NO.
What I really didn't know was how to
CREATE MY OWN OPPORTUNITIES.

So I joined many of them.
I thought the answer had to be YES.
Or at least MAYBE.

I spent tons of money on the latest
get rich quick scheme
and it was costing me my life!

Or the happy life I could have had!

Instead of coming up with my own
original thoughts and ideas,
I relied on others to help me make it big.

I denied my own creativity. What a
RIDICULOUS WASTE!

Pretending that I had the answers and had just found the 'right opportunity' was a

SHAM!

A RIDICULOUS FAÇADE
that fooled only me.

In a silly attempt to escape
my confusion and misery…

I engaged in even more
self-destructive activities….

Too many and quite frankly,
too embarrassing to expound on here.

Deep down inside I was scared
that someone might find out who
I REALLY WAS.

Then they might not want to be my friend or like me,
or even love the **REAL ME.**

My checkered past haunted me.

A RIDICULOUS KIND OF HELL.

The ball and chain of the past
affected all of my decisions.

I labored over my
RIDICULOUS PAST
while the beautiful present passed me by.

I was blind to the bigger picture and
'the other' had such a stronghold on me,
I couldn't Speak, Hear or See for myself.

I blindly accepted and promoted *'the others'*

RIDICULOUS ATTITUDES,
BELIEFS AND OPINIONS

as my own.

I HAD A BRAIN BUT I DIDN'T USE IT!

It was like I had put my brain in a jar on the shelf.
I was walking around with an empty head
that could be filled with anything!

I was
RIDICULOUSLY GULLIBLE.

Not a day went by that I didn't want to
run away and escape.

I even contemplated
ENDING IT ALL.

Chapter 2

Self-Awareness

Then one day I heard a story about an eagle
who thought he was a chicken.

The king of all birds?
**You can't get more RIDICULOUS
than that!**

O-MI-GOD!

That eagle was me!
I had power but I didn't know it.

Suddenly I realized just
HOW RIDICULOUS
I had become.

I let *'the other'* run my life.

I began to realize the impact of who I was being –

AND THE IMPACT ON OTHERS!
OMG.

Like the eagle, I too was confused
about who I truly was.

Listening to *'the other'* caused me to create
a little jail cell of my own making!

The Truth is:
Just like the eagle, I was really

BIG

but had been living
and accepting myself as
small.

I realized that
until I embraced my true self,
I would never be free!

Then a familiar voice from
an old teacher rang out and asked
Two Timeless Questions:

Who I am is a Powerful Person and
what I want is to live purposefully
and be fully self-expressed
and live a life of contribution!

It was time to let my guard down
and just be myself.

I'm ready to quit with the
RIDICULOUS ACT
of mine and start
LIVING AUTHENTICALLY!

I could finally see that I had been
blinded and held hostage by lots of
RIDICULOUS PROGRAMMING!

Self-doubt and the tricks and lies of *'the other'*
had been killing off my beautiful possibilities.

Listening to this ridiculous voice
was equal to giving myself
PERMISSION TO FAIL!

I came to realize that
FAILIURE IS SIMPLY RIDICULOUS!

And then I heard the voice of another teacher say…

"THE PAST DOESN'T EXIST MY DEAR.
THE POWER IS IN THIS PRESENT MOMENT,
RIGHT HERE AND RIGHT NOW."

Then asked...

YES!

I decided to forgive everything and everyone and

LIGMO!

Let It Go - Move On!

Now I see that I have a choice –
I can listen to *'the other'*
or I can put my foot down and say:

Chapter 3

Self-Correction

It was time to
FACE THE MUSIC.

I was ready to
take responsibility for my life and
put an end to my simply ridiculous life-style.

I knew what had to be done…

I started out by giving up my
NEED TO BE RIGHT.

I cleaned up my act by
MAKING AMENDS
with my family and friends.

I asked everyone for forgiveness for my
SHENANIGANS.

First I **FORGAVE MYSELF.**

Then I **FORGAVE OTHERS** for old hurts.

It felt so good, I finally realized that
**FORGIVENESS IS THEY KEY TO
EVERYTHING!**

I felt my heart expanding as I let go of old grievances
and my old judgments of others.

Now that I'm getting over my ridiculous self
I can stop with the charade of
looking good, faking it and pretending!

I am no longer dominated by *'the other'*
nor do I dominate and manipulate others
with my <u>dukkha</u> and ridiculous behaviors.

I've expanded my thinking and I've let go of the past.
Now I'm free to create a real and meaningful life
filled with love for myself!

Good riddance
to my old chicken-like ways!

I said "Good-byë" to the voice of
'the other' who told me:

- I don't fit in.

- No one will take me serious.

- I'm not smart enough.

- I'm not good enough.

- They won't like me.

- I'll be a laughing stock.

Now I say "Hello" to my
new possibilities of:

I decided to become the
person I've always wanted to be.

By expanding my thinking,
I'm letting my natural brilliance shine!

*(although 'the other' tries to frighten me,
warning me that things might be too risky.)*

I realize that I cannot get rid of *'the other'*
and now that I'm aware of its' antics,
I simply choose to let it go, move on
and take the high road.

Now I make powerful choices and
I remind myself daily…

This may seem like a

ridiculous question but

Now What?

Chapter 4

Self-Acceptance

When life's challenges come-a-calling
(and they do),
I simply say:

ANOTHER FABULOUS
GROWTH OPPORTUNITY!

Here's what I've learned to do…

I forgive myself for living inside of
ridiculous stories of the past
and repeating old, worn-out
messages and scripts in my head and
simply ridiculous unconscious behaviors.

I have compassion for myself and
willingness to forgive myself for what I
bought into because I didn't know differently!

Now I realize I have a choice and I'm not a victim!

I've learned to ask myself these questions:

- Am I being authentic or playing some ridiculous game?
- Who Am I being?
- What am I intending to create?
- What new possibilities can I create today?
- What is my part in all of this?
- What am I to learn from this?
- What would Love do?

I realized that I had been looking at what was
bad and wrong instead of what's good.

Now I consider things differently and ask:

What's good about
THIS SITUATION?

What's good about
THIS DAY?

What's good about
ME?

I don't let a day go by without
honoring and loving my Higher Self.

**I practice Gratitude,
Gorgiveness and Lovingness.**

I'm learning to be beautiful
from the inside out!

Now I breathe, relax and
enjoy the ridiculous nature of this life and
not take things too seriously…

**With an open heart,
I smile more and
I stress less!**

To do anything else is

SIMPLY RIDICULOUS!

Word of Caution

It's probably NOT a good idea to read this book and then start pointing out the ridiculous behaviors of others. That might be proof of your own ridiculousness and may not be received well. (see Finger-pointing and Holding on to the need to be right).

This book is a self-help book. **We change the world by changing ourselves.** As we share our growth with others and laugh at our own ridiculous beliefs and past, we can support others as they begin to gently look at their own ridiculous stuff and then choose to let it go.

I decided to laugh at myself first in a humorous way as I healed my wounded child and released the past. I invite you to do the same. Others will soon join in and before you know it, those in your community will all lovingly remind one another to LIGMO!

Remember, we're all having the human experience and it's easier to laugh about it together than cry about it alone.

Imagine a world with no more finger-pointing, blaming, judging, making others bad and wrong and holding on to the need to be right. Wow!

You can make a difference if you want to and your contribution helps and I know you really want to join me and help make this a reality.

It has been said that the harvest is great and the

workers are few. If you're reading this, I'm sure you are one who loves to be part of the solution and are a worker or a healer in our world.

Personal Note from St. Claire

None of us can go on to higher levels of achievement and realize our inherent genius ability until we stop the ridiculous madness that keeps us living small and separated from one another.

It has been said that there is no one true path, only one true destination and each of us must go through our own individual process to find that ultimate truth.

I'm still doing the work on all levels - daily! That's the way it is. Life's journey is one of continuous flowering and unfolding. I've had many incredible enlightened teachers and each has helped to open my eyes to incredible possibilities. It's up to me to choose.

If you're interested in knowing more about the tools I use, on the next page is a short list of seminars, self-study courses, books and movies that have helped me to de-program myself and begin to positively re-program myself over the years. Don't take my word for anything, check it out for yourself!

I DARE YOU to Let Go of your Ridiculous Self and live Powerfully and Beautifully!

Letting Go of all of your Dukkha (suffering, drama and negativity) is strangely and wonderfully liberating!

Programs that have positively changed my life for the better. *Blessings and Gratitude to all of them.*

- Self-Realization Fellowship
- A Course in Miracles
- The Institute of HeartMath
- The Sedona Method
- LandMark Education
- Vipassana Mediation
- Accelerated Learning
- NLP Course Work
- Learning Strategies.com
- Many other spiritual works…

A few books that changed my life
- Think and Grow Rich, Napolean Hill
- Power versus Force, Dr. David Hawkins
- The HeartMath Solution, Doc Childre
- Three Magic Words, US Anderson
- The Greatest Miracle in The World, Og Mandino
- The Biology of Transcendence, Joseph Chilton Pearce

Powerful Life-Changing Movies
- Pay it Forward
- What the Bleep Do We Know
- What Dreams May Come

Working on YOUR Stuff

The vast majority of humans all have some *ridiculous stuff* going on inside of our hearts and heads that needs to be healed and released.

The pages that follow are designed for personal reflections. After all, this book was just a humorous way to kill some time if you're not ready to work on our own ridiculousness, true? True.

I encourage you to go back through the book and take note of the things that remind you the most of YOUR ridiculous stuff. Don't forget about the ones I didn't mention here. These were mine; yours may be similar and you may have some different ones. Share and Purge!

Lighten up, have fun and laugh at it all as you gently learn to LIGMO! Let It Go and Move On!

If the work I do interests you, Simply Ridiculous can be presented as a workshop series or breakout or keynote for any special event. My programs are perfect to address the concerns of negative attitude, conflict, teambuilding and leadership, change, stress, dealing with difficult people, self-esteem, diversity, racism, violence, inspiration and humor. This work is about healing those conditions and uplifting our brothers and sisters of humanity everywhere.

LIGMO offers special peer education program for schools or clubs. Join the LIGMO Movement of everyone that is committed to eradicating ridiculous beliefs and behaviors.

We need all the help we can get with this Movement!

I also have awesome gifts and products that you will like at www.LIGMO.com They are designed to serve as continual reminders to Let It Go and Move On – to your higher good where you belong.

The Moment of Truth

They say the truth will set you free and I say; *Yes, the truth will set you free, but no one said it would be pretty.*

How easy it is to look at the illustrations in this book and point to the behaviors of people we know. It's easier to see these things in others than in ourselves, isn't it? Yep.

I believe that the one who tells the truth gets free and you know deep down inside that can't heal what you can't feel so instead of denying your dukkha, just tell the truth, laugh about it, let it go and move on.

You'll liberate yourself and others and soon you will find yourself feeling as light as a feather…

On the following pages are a few questions. Take some quality time with yourself and answer these simple questions.

I've told the truth, now it's your turn! But only if you're bold and ready to let go of the ridiculous…

List YOUR Top 3 Ridiculous Beliefs or Behaviors

1. _____

_____

_____

_____

2. _____

_____

_____

_____

3. _____

_____

_____

_____

List 3 Ridiculous Messages from *'the other'* you're ready to let of and be free from:

1. _____

_____

_____

_____

2. _____

_____

_____

_____

3. _____

_____

_____

_____

List 3 Steps you can and will take to begin cleaning up your act immediately!

1. _____

_____

_____

_____

2. _____

_____

_____

_____

3. _____

_____

_____

_____

TIMELESS WISDOM
from a Favorite Teacher

"Life should be chiefly service. Without that idea, the intelligence that God has given you is not reaching out towards its goal. When in service you forget the little self, you will feel the big Self of Spirit.

As the vital rays of the sun nurture all, so should you spread rays of hope in the hearts of the poor and forsaken, kindle courage in the hearts of the despondent and light a new strength in the hearts of those who
think that they are failures.

When you realize that life is a joyous battle of duty and at the same time a passing dream, and when you become filled with the joy of making others happy by giving them kindness and peace, in God's eyes, your life is a success."

-Paramahansa Yogananda
Hindu Teacher and Master

Ask yourself, "Who Am I?"

1. _____

_____

_____

_____

2. _____

_____

_____

_____

3. _____

_____

_____

_____

Ask yourself, "What do I want to be – to do – to have?"

1. _____

_____

_____

2. _____

_____

_____

3. _____

_____

_____

Affirm: I resolve to become the person I've always wanted to be!

My new self-talk starts with these affirmations:

1. _____

_____

_____

2. _____

_____

_____

3. _____

_____

_____

A Continuous Journey...

In this book, MeMe began her journey. Self–Awareness is the first step, the second is Emotinal–Management and the third is Personal–Mastery.

In future books, you'll see MeMe confront other issues such as violence, racism, and being the best learner possible as she expands as a GHB – a Growing Human Being!

Join MeMe as she continues to grow in life's ever expanding journey!

Important Life Principles

The Three LIGMO Life Principles are:

1. **Self–Awareness**: In this process of self-exploration, you'll come to understand clearly and admit, without judgment, your own ridiculous, unbecoming attitudes and behaviors. You'll realize the impact of your own negative internal and external communication, on yourself, and on others. You'll be challenged to take responsibility for your every thought, word and deed.

2. **Emotional–Management**: Cleaning up your act and working on your stuff means learning to use the tools of self-management, self-discipline, self-correction and self-respect. You'll learn to clean up the ridiculous immediately and Let It Go and Move on!

3. **Personal–Mastery**: Personal–Mastery is about a commitment to master the intellect through life-long learning and developing emotional and spiritual intelligence and activating the wisdom of your heart. LIGMO Personal–Mastery represents continuous expansion and a life of outstanding contribution to the world around you.

Find out more at www.LIGMO.com.

Cool Ways to Share this Book

Use the previous *"Working on Your Stuff"* pages to start the process of LIGMO!

GIVE a copy of this book to those in your organization, department, family or group. Once everyone stops their ridiculousness, harmony and productivity will increase by leaps and bounds. Who wouldn't want that?

GIFT someone you really love a copy. As they struggle with their humanity, it could be the best thing they ever laugh at! Laughter is a healing medicine so remember to laugh, heal and LIGMO together!

HIRE Millicent for an unforgettable Simply Ridiculous Workshop or Keynote at your next meeting, convention or special event.

ASK about the LIGMO Workshop Series for Personal and Professional Development.

GET an Accountability Partner. It's cool to have someone you trust to check in with and ask, *"Am I being Ridiculous?"* The goal is to be humorously and lovingly reminded to LIGMO! Heal the world and make it fun by laughing at it – starting with yourself. Humor is Divine!

You want Personal Freedom

If you've read this far, you're ready to go to the next level because what you really want is Personal Freedom.

LIGMO is a Guided Self-Help Coaching Program that provides a variety of educational programs and resources to help you learn how to let go of old, worn out, reactionary and wounded behaviors and live the life you really want and deserve!

We help you help yourself!

This program is filled with principles and practical exercises to learn the three Principles of LIGMO: Self-Awareness; Emotional-Management, and ultimately Personal-Mastery.

Getting free is entirely up to you!

You will be exposed to many different resources and disciplines to help make LIGMO an active part of your daily life-style and to start experiencing the Personal Freedom that you deserve.

Take action today!
Visit freedom@ligmo.com to get signed up for one of my free webinars; share your thoughts on the blog posts; and join the movement! Often we heal ourselves by engaging with and helping others. No more pity party!

You are also welcome to send me a personal email to freedom@ligmo.com. We can chat about your goals and dreams and how to clear the path so that you can experience the life and love you deserve.

**This message is perfect for
Women and Faith Based Communities....**

People don't need another revival, they need training:
More than ever, people are in need of training to develop skills to deal with today's conflicts and stressors. Women especially rave about this honest and candid conversation as it opens the door to discuss sensitive issues that aren't easily approached.

St. Claire gives unforgettable Keynotes at:
- Spiritual Conferences
- Women's Organizations
- Special and Customized Events

The LIGMO Seminars teaches your members:
- Self-Awareness: How to begin to admit that they need help on their healing journey.
- What to do: When stuck in psychological and emotional mud, options aren't always obvious. Sometimes we need a bit of coaching from a non-judgmental outside source to help see the light.
- Form a new vision of self: Often we need to create a new vision of ourselves and focus on creating a purposeful life, filled with joy and contribution.
- Learn to tell the truth: Denial and pride keep us stuck in lower levels of consciousness. Every day is a good day to let go of denial and pride.
- Protocols for Letting Go: It's easy to say, *"Let it go and move on"* and yet we all know it takes

practice, reminders and practical, easy to use tools to help make that happen. Participants develop life skills which help them disengage from the ridiculous and really move on to experience joy and freedom in their lives.

Book a training opportunity for your church or non-profit at freedom@ligmo.com.

Believe it or not –
People bring their Ridiculousness to Work!

Since our personal and professional lives overlap, and personal problems affect professional productivity, smart employers invest in personal development training to help their employees deal with the ridiculous stressors of life.

Bringing in LIGMO could be the best investment your company could ever make for your employees.

LIGMO trainings help:
- Deal with stressful and sensitive issues
- Cut down on unnecessary conflict and drama
- Improve internal and external communication
- Create a new culture of respect
- Increase productivity and outcomes
- Help your employees see new options
- Encourage your team to be their best selves while they stay focused on the mission

LIGMO provides outstanding training for businesses that will leave a positive and lasting impression on your employees. Our programs help you transform the hearts, minds of everyone in your business and eliminate excuses!

Send an email today to freedom@ligmo.com to set up an interview too find out more about the LIGMO (Let It Go Move On) Seminar Series for Personal and Professional Development.

**Ready to create LIGMO Facilitators
Inside of your Organization?**

Sponsor a Train The Trainer Opportunity
We will gladly deliver an outstanding training at your
business, teaching your employees how to LIGMO.

And we can do better than that – You could have a
special team trained inside of your business to deliver
the LIGMO program and help reinforce the 3
Principles of LIGMO: Self-Awareness; Emotional
Management and Personal Mastery; and other simple
and valuable life lessons.

Contact us today to set up an interview for a needs
assessment and schedule your training. Email:
freedom@ligmo.com.

Join the LIGMO Movement!

If you would like to be part of something bigger than yourself, or share your transformation and how this message has positively impacted you, please visit LIGMO at:

- FBook www.facebook.com/ligmo-letitgomoveon
- Twitter twitter.com/ligmo
- In-gram instagram.com/ligmolady
- Pintrest pinterest.com/ligmo
- Be bold and share your freedom without judgment using the LIGMO hashtag #ligmo

Join the LIGMO Movement!
Set an example first: Tell the truth and get free by letting go of the pain of the past and move on and help others do the same!

Get Your Cool LIGMO Stuff!
Visit www.LIGMOStore.com to check out the cool LIGMO Customized T-shirts and other products! LIGMO is not just a message to wear but something to live into daily.

Millicent St. Claire!

Seasoned Seminar Leader, Inspirational Speaker and Author, Millicent St. Claire uses her groundbreaking book *Negativity and Drama is Simply Ridiculous!* and the *Three Principles of LIGMO!* to help business professionals, women and  students let go of self-limiting beliefs and behaviors and have a new experience of themselves.

As a LIGMO Luminary *(one who walks in the light and releases daily)*, St. Claire shares how to LET GO of everything that is *Simply Ridiculous* and focus on what's really important in life – personal and professional development so that you can stand out, achieve your goals and make a positive contribution in this life.

This LIGMO Luminary has a friendly, animated and girlish style that just might surprise you as she opens hearts and minds in a lighthearted and magical way. Clients rave about their personal insights and breakthroughs and you will too.

St. Claire travels extensively, speaking and training at businesses, organizations, and colleges, public workshops and private coaching.

To inquire about coaching or bring St. Claire to your upcoming event or conference, send details to freedom@ligmo.com

Live! Love! Learn! Laugh! LIGMO!

LIGMO!

Let It Go. Move On!

LIGMO isn't just something cute to say. Letting go is an ongoing process and a positive lifestyle that leads to Personal Freedom.

30133054R00066

Made in the USA
Charleston, SC
06 June 2014